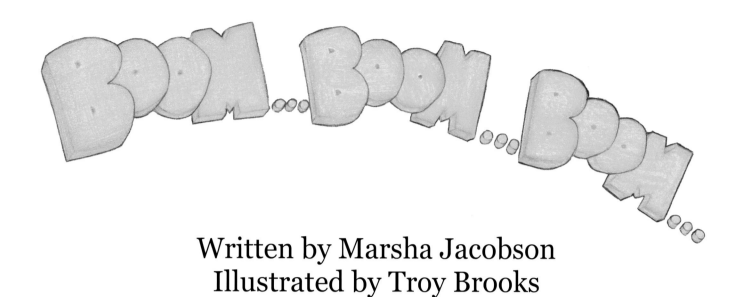

Written by Marsha Jacobson
Illustrated by Troy Brooks

for Russell, Ilan, Adam, Dustin and Gabi
my sanctuary, my love

Full of Ideas Publishing

There are some people I would like to thank who have helped me immeasurably with the creation of this book: Gaurav Puri—for his meticulous eye for detail, for his brilliant mind, but mostly for his kind heart. Robyn Jacobson—for her hours of selfless editing and for changing from red to black ink. Miriam, my mother—for instilling in me a love of storytelling with her Fairy Jo-Jo stories. Dalya and Batia, my sisters—for allowing me to test the waters in a safe place, for their unconditional love and their rose-tinted admiration. Sandy and Michelle, my sisters—although far, always close to my heart. Shirley Sklar—for her constant and consistent affirmation.
- *Marsha Jacobson*


Everything I have put into this special project I would like to dedicate to my beautiful Mother, who not only taught me how to draw, but gave me the incredible bedrock that comes from true unconditional love.
- *Troy Brooks*

Library and Archives Canada Cataloguing in Publication

Jacobson, Marsha, 1957-
    Boom-- boom-- boom / Marsha Jacobson, Troy Brooks.

(Feel ease series)
Also available in electronic format.
ISBN 978-1-926561-20-2

    1. Emotional intelligence--Juvenile literature.  I. Brooks, Troy
II. Title.  III. Series: Jacobson, Marsha, 1957- .  Feel ease series.
BF149.5.J33 2008       j152.4       C2008-905767-8

Full of Ideas Publishing
P.O. Box 32562
RPO Village Gate
Richmond Hill, Ontario
L4C 0A2
Canada

# Note to
# Parents and Caregivers

This story will be beneficial if read independently by your child or with your involvement. Reading this story with your child will strongly reinforce the messages in it. As a parent or caregiver, there are many subtle ways in which you can do this.

## Answer...

... all your child's questions with honesty, particularly when they are about negative feelings. Often, our initial reaction is to console, explain or eliminate negative feelings. This does not provide your child with the tools to deal with similar situations in the future.

For example, if a child expresses fear in response to something in the book, avoid reactions like, "There's nothing to be afraid of," or, "Don't be scared." This makes your child feel unheard and shuts down communication. Accepting all of your child's feelings, allows your child to accept their own feelings and work with them.

## Explore...

... with your child how they feel about different parts of the book. Encourage them to talk about experiences that may be triggered by reading the book. Listen with patience, interest and accept without judgement. Some useful questions could be, "I wonder how she felt when...?" or, "Does that remind you of anything?" or, "Have you ever felt that way?"

## Share...

... your own feelings and relevant experiences. Children love to hear feeling stories from adults. Make sure they know that your story does not replace theirs. Start by saying, "That must have felt _____ for you. When I was little..." or, "That's a really interesting way of looking at that. It reminds me of..." Once you are finished, ask your child for their comments.

## Expand...

... your child's vocabulary of feeling words. A *Feeling Vocabulary* is provided to assist you at the back of the book. A greater feeling vocabulary is correlated with a higher emotional intelligence. In this story, more complicated feeling words are purposely introduced to stretch your child's vocabulary.

## Enjoy...

... reading and sharing this book with your child!

"Mommy... MOMMY...
MOMMEEEEEE!" screamed Gabi.

Mommy raced into Gabi's room and
found her sitting straight up in bed. She
looked terrified.

"What is it, sweetie?" Mommy asked
gently. "Did you have a bad dream?"

"There were monsters... I was running... and... and... I couldn't find you!" Gabi cried.

Gabi looked very afraid. Her eyes were big and round. Even her eyebrows had scrunched into a deep frown.

Mommy replied, "Oh no! Monsters are so frightening. That must have been very scary for you." She climbed into Gabi's bed and curled up with her.

Gabi wrapped her arms and legs around Mommy and clung to her. Mommy hugged Gabi very, very tightly.

"I'm here now. You've found me," Mommy added quietly.

They snuggled together for a while. Mommy held Gabi and stroked her hair.

Suddenly, Gabi sat up and whispered urgently, "Mommy, do you hear that?"

"What, sweetie?" Mommy asked.

"That noise," Gabi's voice was louder now. "It sounds like *boom... boom... boom...* Do you hear it?"

"I... don't... think so," Mommy said hesitantly, "but what do you think it is?"

Gabi looked around the room quickly. "I don't know, Mommy. But I'm scared! Are you sure you can't hear it?"

Mommy answered tenderly, "No, I can't sweetheart, but I can see you're very frightened. Where do you think the noise is coming from?"

"I don't know," Gabi replied. "The closet? Yes! I think it's coming from the closet, Mommy!"

Mommy climbed out of bed,
and gently took Gabi's hand. Gabi
pulled back, feeling too afraid to leave her bed.

She said, "No, Mommy, you check. I'll stay right here!"

Mommy understood. She could see that Gabi was too afraid to even move.

In a calm but firm voice she said, "Come sweetheart. I know you're scared. Let's check the closet together."

Clinging to Mommy's hand, Gabi walked cautiously towards the closet. She felt certain that something was going to jump out at them. She crept behind Mommy.

While Mommy opened the door very slowly, Gabi held her breath and peeked from behind... and... and...

... there was nothing.

Gabi let out her breath with a big *whooshing* sound.

Jumping back onto her bed, Gabi clutched her blanket. She watched closely as Mommy searched her room.

Mommy looked under the bed...

... behind the curtains

and behind every toy bin.

Mommy even looked
in the drawers.

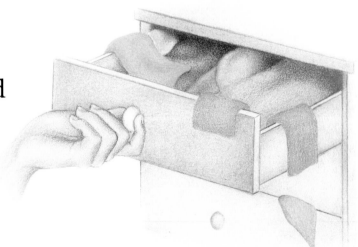

"Mommy, where do you think that *boom... boom... boom...* is coming from?" asked Gabi.

Mommy wished she could hear the sound so that she could answer Gabi's question. Mommy listened carefully and thought she could hear a small sound.

"Maybe Dusty left his TV on!"

Mommy felt excited at this idea, but then they looked at each other, realizing that there could be a problem.

Dusty was Gabi's older teenage brother and the one thing that he hated was being woken up. How were they going to check his room without waking him?

Boom... Boom... Boom...

Mommy took charge. "OK, this is what we are going to do. Let's find your flashlight and creep into Dusty's room." Gabi did not have to be told twice. She knew that Dusty would not be happy if he was woken up!

Gabi knew exactly where her flashlight was. It was inside Squishy.

Squishy was Gabi's backpack!

Squishy was important to Gabi because her grandmother had given it to her for her third birthday. She had loved it ever since and took it everywhere. It was home to all of Gabi's important stuff. Mommy had named her backpack Squishy because even when it seemed completely full, Gabi somehow managed to squish more things in.

Gabi grabbed Squishy from next to her bed. She had a sense of urgency now.

Almost climbing into Squishy, she began searching.

"I've got it!" she exclaimed, proudly showing Mommy her flashlight.

Gabi put Squishy on her back and turned on the flashlight. Together, Mommy and Gabi left the bedroom.

It felt like the start of a scary adventure.

As Mommy's hand reached for the doorknob to Dusty's room, Gabi hesitated for a moment. "What if we wake him?" she whispered to Mommy.

Boom...
Boom...
Boom...

The sound grew louder.

Mommy said quietly, "Would you rather not go, sweetheart?"

"No, we have to check!" Gabi replied with determination.

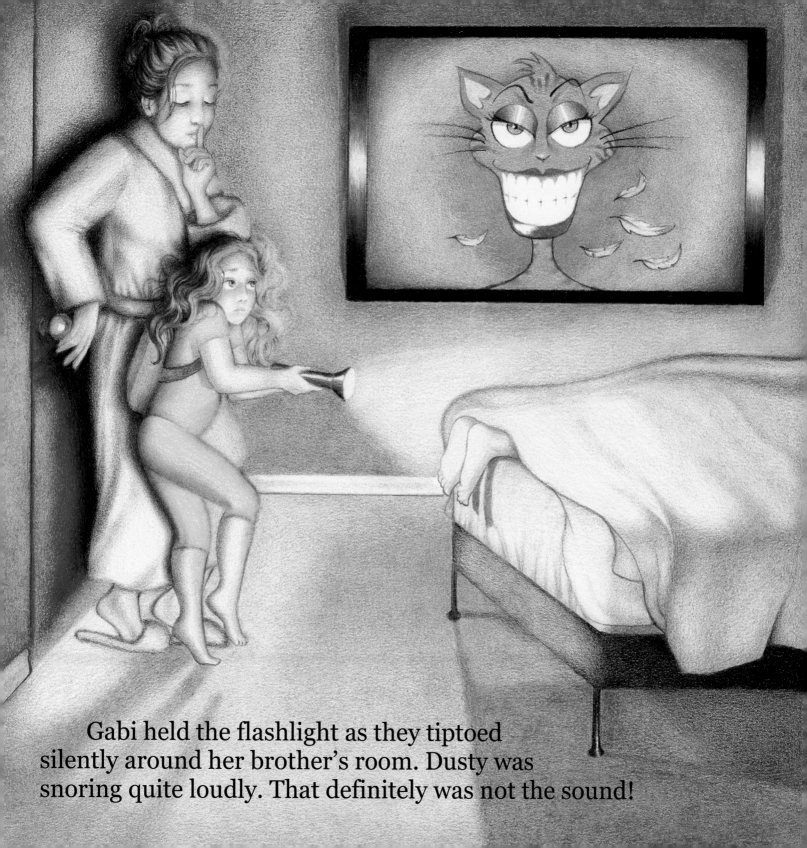

Gabi held the flashlight as they tiptoed
silently around her brother's room. Dusty was
snoring quite loudly. That definitely was not the sound!

Suddenly, Dusty stopped snoring.

Mommy and Gabi had the same thought, "Oh no!"

Gabi hid the flashlight under her nightshirt and they both stood very still, petrified, waiting to see what would happen.

Dusty let out a big snort and they both went, "Phew!"

Gabi pulled Mommy down to her and whispered in her ear, "Let's get out of here!"

Mommy and Gabi moved quickly towards Dusty's door.

On the way out, Mommy turned off the TV. Gabi stuffed her flashlight into Squishy.

They stood outside Dusty's room and pressed their ears against his door.

"It seems quiet in there, Gabi. Do *you* still hear the sound?" Mommy asked.

Boom... Boom... Boom...

"I can still hear it, Mommy.
It's really loud. Maybe it's coming from
the kitchen."

She ran down the stairs, flipping on the light
switches wherever she could. She held Mommy's hand,
but Mommy noticed she wasn't holding it quite as tightly.

When they arrived at the kitchen, Gabi switched on all the lights. She let go of Mommy's hand, but stayed close.

They looked everywhere. Under the kitchen table, beside the fridge, behind the garbage bin, inside ALL the cupboards and even in the sink!

"Definitely not here." Gabi was disappointed.

Boom... Boom... Boom...

"Let's try the living room!" suggested Gabi. There were a lot more places to look in this room.

They searched under the chairs, behind the couches, in the planters and inside the cabinet. Then, Gabi noticed a big vase on top of a high table.

Gabi wondered if the noise could be coming from inside there.

She had to find out! She climbed onto the couch beside the table. Very slowly and carefully, she peered into the vase. Nothing there!

"Getting down will be easy," she thought as she turned to jump onto the floor. In that moment she had forgotten about the vase and her elbow gave it a big bump. The vase wobbled this way and then it wobbled that way, but Gabi managed to grab it just before it fell.

"Oh gosh, that was close!" Gabi felt relieved.

BOOM... BOOM... BOOM...

"I hear it. It's so loud, Mommy. It has to be somewhere!" Gabi felt aggravated.

"Aargh! I'm going to try the laundry room, Mommy!" said Gabi, already moving in that direction.

"Oh no, not the laundry room," whispered Mommy to herself.

With all the tiny spaces in that room AND with all the mess, she knew she had to prepare herself for a long search!

Mommy thought it would really help if she could hear that sound. She was frustrated and was feeling quite perplexed.

Gabi was already buried in the laundry basket. As she climbed out, a pair of Dusty's jeans dangled from her head. She blurted out desperately, "Mommy, I just can't find it!"

"It really is frustrating when you can't find something that you're looking for. Especially when you're trying so hard," Mommy replied.

Gabi stopped for a minute. "You're right, I do feel frustrated!" She felt very frustrated!

Mommy was thinking very hard. She definitely could not hear any sound but really wanted to know what Gabi was hearing.

Mommy sat down on a pile of soft clothing. Her heart was beating very quickly from all the rushing.

She sat up straight as a thought popped into her head. She wondered if... if... could it be...?

"Gabi, sweetheart, could we sit quietly and talk about something?"

"What?" Gabi asked impatiently.

Mommy hugged Gabi and gently pulled her close. She put her ear against Gabi's chest. "Hmmm... would you mind doing something, Gabi?" she asked.

"What?" Gabi did not understand and she felt irritated.

Mommy said, "Listen to my chest and tell me if you hear something." Gabi thought this was very strange, but now she was very curious and did as Mommy asked.

B O O M… B O O M… B O O M…

"That's the noise, Mommy! But… But… how can I hear it? What *is* it?"

"That's the sound of my heart beating in my chest. But  sweetheart, I think the *boom… boom… boom…* you are hearing is your heartbeat, not mine." Gabi looked confused. "Sometimes when we're anxious, our hearts beat very loudly and we can hear them in our ears." Mommy continued.

"What does anxious mean?" Gabi asked with a puzzled look on her face.

"It's another word for scared or frightened," Mommy replied. "Tonight you were very anxious because you had a very scary nightmare. When you woke up you felt so afraid that your heart was beating very loudly. It was so loud that you could hear it and that made you feel even more anxious! I think I would have felt that way too."

Mommy's explanation felt right to Gabi. She had definitely felt anxious from that awful nightmare!

Suddenly, Gabi realized that she couldn't hear the noise anymore. Now that she and Mommy knew what that sound was, it just disappeared. "Wow, it's gone!" Gabi told Mommy with a big smile on her face.

Smiling back at her, Mommy explained, "Yes, it's true. It really helps to know what you're feeling and it helps even more to share it."

Together, they left the laundry room. "We'll clean up the mess in the morning," Mommy said sleepily.

They climbed the stairs, switching off the lights as they went. They returned back to Gabi's bed and lay quietly for a few minutes. Slowly, Gabi's eyes closed.

When Gabi was breathing gently and peacefully, Mommy kissed her softly on the forehead and, as quiet as a mouse, she left the room.

As Mommy closed Gabi's bedroom door, she
whispered, "Good night, my angel."

# FEELING VOCABULARY

The following is a list of feeling and feeling-related words found within this story.

Parents and caregivers are encouraged to discuss these words and phrases with their child. As a starting point, ensure that your child understands the meanings of the words. Conversations can then expand into exciting discoveries about other feelings and feelings in general. You may also want to introduce your child to the idea that feelings vary in intensity. For example, "On a scale of 1 to 10, how _____ are you?"

Expanding on the story will allow wonderful opportunities for adults and children to explore how they feel.

A good repertoire of words to describe feelings is key to developing high emotional intelligence, as learning the alphabet is to language.

*(as they appear in the story)*

| | | |
|---|---|---|
| screamed | could be a problem | perplexed |
| terrified | hated | blurted out |
| gently | took charge | desperately |
| bad dream | not happy | frustrating |
| cried | loved | very frustrated |
| very afraid | sense of urgency | impatiently |
| deep frown | proudly | irritated |
| frightening | scary adventure | curious |
| very scary | hesitated | confused |
| urgently | determination | anxious |
| scared | "Oh no!" | puzzled |
| very frightened | petrified | so afraid |
| too afraid | "Phew!" | felt right |
| calm | disappointed | a big smile |
| cautiously | relieved | share |
| felt certain | aggravated | feeling |
| felt excited | frustrated | peacefully |